Fifty Easy Classical Guitar Pieces

Arranged and edited by **Jerry Willard**.

PLAYBACK+
Speed • Pitch • Balance • Loop

To access companion recorded performances online, visit:
www.halleonard.com/mylibrary
Enter Code
6998-4536-2359-0789

Cover photography by Randall Wallace
Project editor: Peter Pickow

ISBN: 978-0-8256-2827-6

HAL•LEONARD®

Visit Hal Leonard Online at
www.halleonard.com

Contact us:
Hal Leonard
7777 West Bluemound Road
Milwaukee, WI 53213
Email: info@halleonard.com

In Europe, contact:
Hal Leonard Europe Limited
42 Wigmore Street
Marylebone, London, W1U 2RN
Email: info@halleonardeurope.com

In Australia, contact:
Hal Leonard Australia Pty. Ltd.
4 Lentara Court
Cheltenham, Victoria, 3192 Australia
Email: info@halleonard.com.au

Contents

Selected Composer Biographies

Fernando Carulli was born in Naples, Italy, on February 10, 1770, the son of a famous statesman. Carulli's first musical instruction was on 'cello; however, he was soon attracted to the guitar. Carulli was entirely self taught as a guitarist, yet he rapidly became known as one of the leading virtuosi of his day. In 1808 he moved to Paris, where he was to make his home for the rest of his life. He was an extremely prolific composer, writing a great number of solos as well as chamber works for the guitar. Carulli died in Paris on February 17, 1841.

Napoleon Coste learned to play guitar from his mother and was teaching and performing on the instrument by the time he was eighteen years old. Born in the eastern French department of Doubs, he made his way to Paris in 1830 where he published his first compositions for guitar in 1840. He was well regarded as a concert performer and his fans even compared him to Fernando Sor. When he was fifty-seven, he suffered a broken arm which prevented him from giving further performances.

Fernando Sor is considered to be the most important nineteenth-century composer of works for the guitar. He was born in Barcelona, Spain on February 2, 1778, the son of a well-to-do Catalan merchant. Sor received his first musical instruction at the monastery of Montserrat. At eighteen, he composed his first opera, *Telemachus on Calypso's Isle*, which was performed in Barcelona in 1797 to tremendous acclaim. In 1812, Sor moved to Paris and established himself as a great guitar virtuoso and composer. It was around this time that the music critic Fétis dubbed him "the Beethoven of the guitar." He made his London début in 1815 to great acclaim, and, in 1820, he moved to Russia where he produced three ballets. In 1830, Sor published his famous *Method pour la Guitar*, one of the finest methods ever written. He died in Paris on July 10, 1839.

Dionisio Aguado was born on April 8, 1784, in Madrid, Spain, and died there on December 20, 1849. He studied music at a college in Madrid where a monk named Basilio taught him guitar and the elements of music. Later on he worked with the renowned singer/guitarist Manuel Garcia, from whom he obtained a thorough knowledge of the resources of the guitar. In 1803 Aguado moved to Aranjuez, where he devoted himself to the further study of the guitar. It was during this period that he developed a system of fingering and harmonic effects that became his *Method*, which was published in Madrid in 1824. Aguado moved to Paris in 1825, where he became friends with the great guitar virtuoso Fernando Sor. In fact, Sor wrote the beautiful "Les deux amis" in celebration of their friendship. In 1838, Aguado returned to Madrid where he spent the remainder of his life.

Gaspar Sanz was born Francisco Bartolome Sanz y Celma on April 4, 1640, near Saragossa, Spain, in the tiny town of Calenda. It was later that he took the name Gaspar. As a member of an old and wealthy family, he was educated at the University of Salamanca where he studied literature and music and received a degree in theology. Sanz was well traveled and spent much time in Italy where he studied guitar with Cristoforo Carisani and Lelio Colista. Sanz acquired such a great reputation as a guitarist and composer that he was appointed guitar teacher to Don Juan of Austria to whom he dedicated his *Instrucción de música sobre la guitarra Española* (published 6 December 1674 in Saragossa, Spain). Sanz left us a great legacy of elegant and sophisticated guitar solos that have been recorded and performed by many of the world's great virtuosos.

John Dowland was born in 1562 and is generally considered the greatest lutenist/composer of the late Renaissance. Dowland traveled a great deal and lived in Denmark, Germany, and Italy, as well as his native England. He is known for his beautiful lute songs and solo lute compositions. Dowland was appointed to the court of James I in 1612, a post he held until his death in 1626.

Robert DeVisee was a French guitarist, viol player, singer, and composer. He was born in the second half of the seventeenth century and died in the early eighteenth century. DeVisee was a chamber musician to Louis XIV, and in 1719 he was appointed guitar teacher to the king. His guitar compositions exploit the instrument's resources to the fullest extent and stand as the premier examples of French Baroque guitar literature.

Mauro Giuliani was born in Bisceglie, Italy, on July 27, 1781. He settled in Vienna in 1806 and became famous as the greatest living guitarist and also as a notable composer. He led the classical guitar movement in Vienna, teaching, performing, and composing a rich repertory. He pioneered modern notation practices for guitar music, notating melody, bass, and inner voices individually on one staff. Giuliani died in Naples on May 8, 1829.

Study No. 2

Dionisio Aguado
(1784–1849)

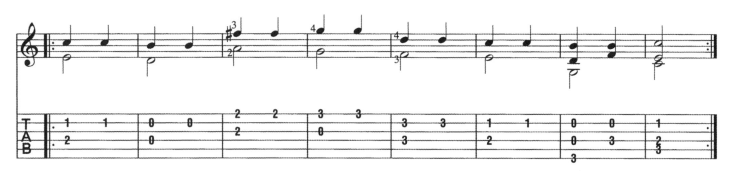

Study

Napoleon Coste
(1806–1883)

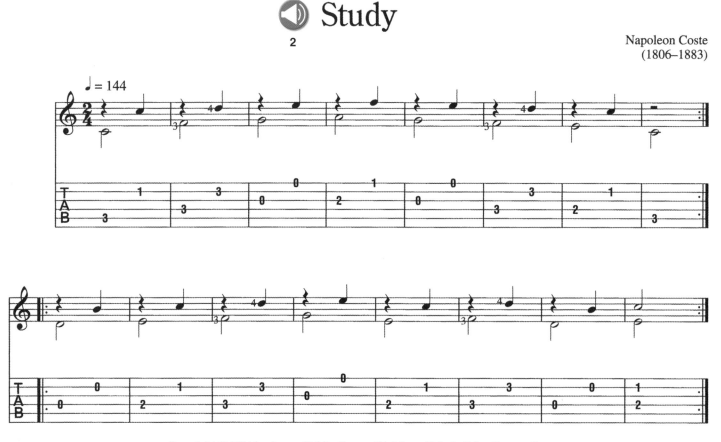

Pastorale

Joseph Küffner
(1776–1856)

Study

Napoleon Coste

Andante No. 1

5

Fernando Sor
(1778-1839)

Study No. 3

Fernando Sor

Moderato ♩ = 108

Toy

Anonymous 16th century
Jane Pickering Lute Manuscript

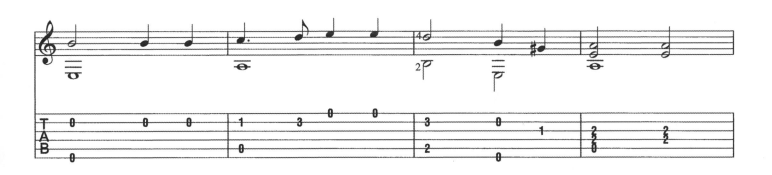

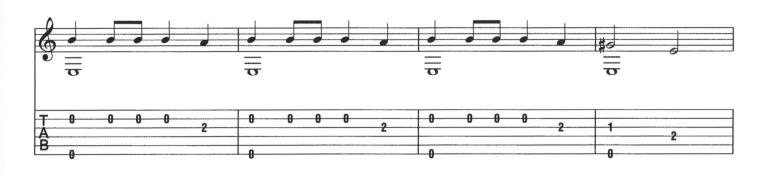

Etude

Dionisio Aguado

Scarborough Fair

English folk song

Andantino

Dionisio Aguado

Study in G Major

11

Napoleon Coste

Study

Napoleon Coste

Ecossaise

Mauro Giuliani
(1781-1829)

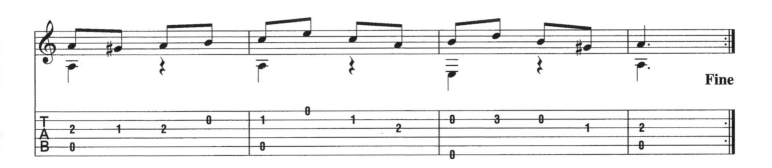

Fine

D.C. al Fine

Andantino

14

Fernando Sor

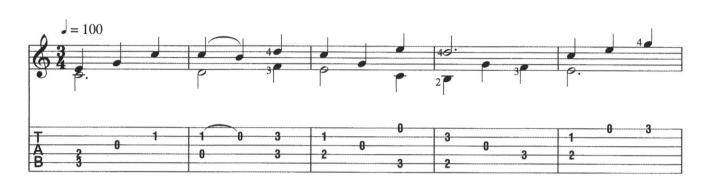

Tanz

15

Georg Leopold Fuhrmann
1615 Testudo Gallo-Germanica

Clarin de los Mosqueteros del Rey de Francia
The Bugle of the French King's Musketeers

Gaspar Sanz
(1640–1710)

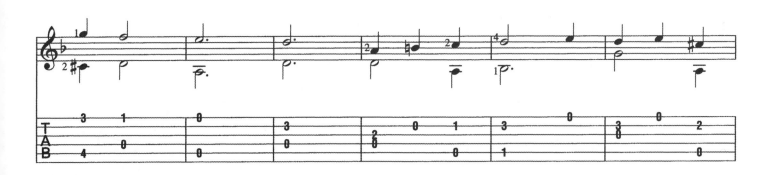

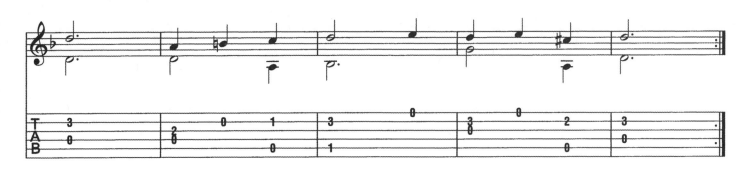

Menuet

Robert DeVisee
(1650–1725)

(II position throughout)

Menuet

18

Dionisio Aguado

Lesson

19

Dionisio Aguado

Landler

20

Joseph Küffner

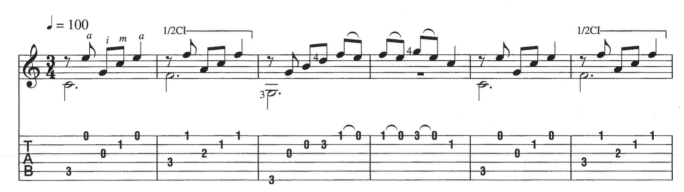

Andantino

21

Ferdinando Carulli
(1770–1841)

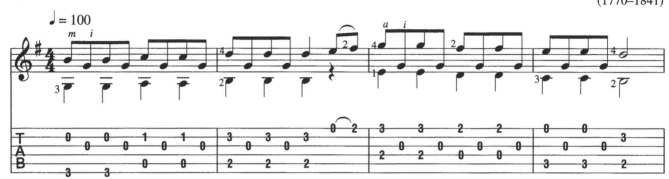

Aria

Johann Anton Logy
(*c.* 1645–1721)

Toy

23

Anonymous 16th century
Jane Pickering Lute Manuscript

Gigue

24

Johann Anton Logy

Orlando Sleepeth

25

John Dowland
(1563–1626)

Bianco Fiore

26

Cesare Negri
(1520–1595)

Andantino

27

Felix Horetzky
(1796–1870)

Dove Son Quei Fieri Occhi?

Anonymous
Italian, 16th century

Sarabande

Johann Anton Logy

Pezzo Tedesco

Anonymous
Italian, 16th century

La Cavalleria de Napoles con dos Clarines

31

Gaspar Sanz

Chorale

J. S. Bach
(1685-1750)

Study

Napoleon Coste

ritard.

a tempo

Study in A Minor

Napoleon Coste

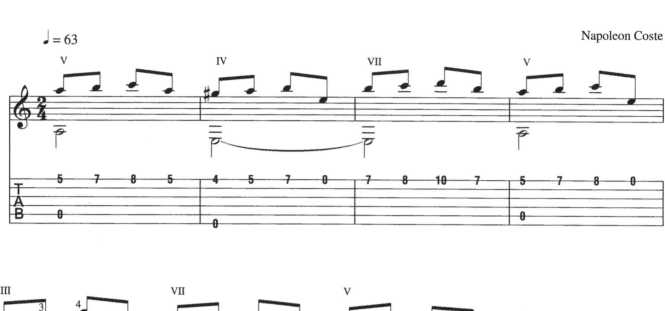

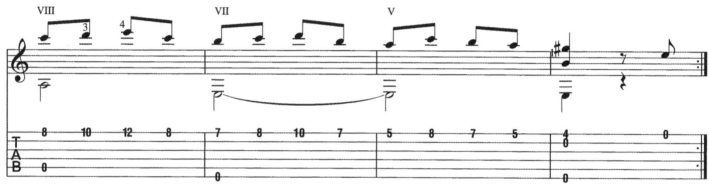

Spagnoletta

35

Anonymous
Italian, 16th century

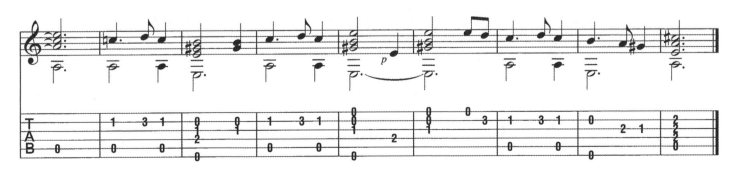

Minuet

36

Anonymous
18th century

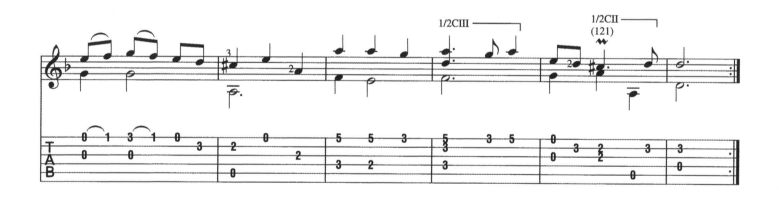

Prelude

37

Robert DeVisee

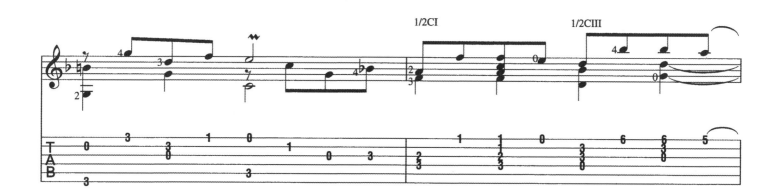

Etude

38

Fernando Sor

Villanos

Gaspar Sanz

Kemp's Jig

Anonymous
English, 16th century

Etude

41

Fernando Sor
Op.35

Minuet

42

J. S. Bach

Etude in A Minor

43

Mauro Giuliani

Etude

44

Fernando Sor
Op. 60, No.8

D.C. al Fine

Humming Song

45

Robert Schumann
(1810–1856)

Moderato ♩ = 100

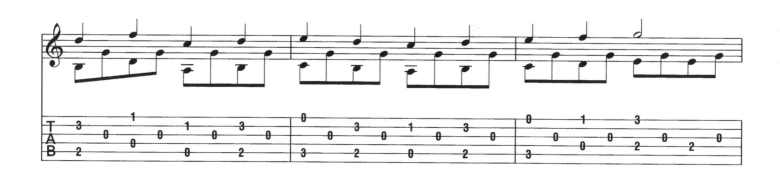

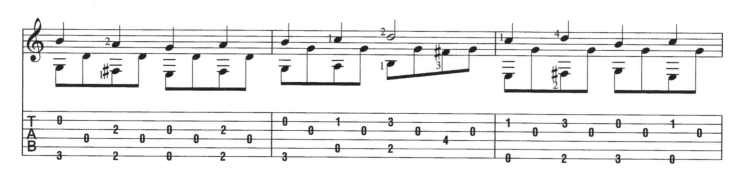

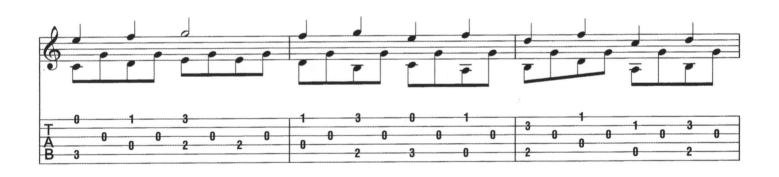

Etude

46

Fernando Sor
Op. 31

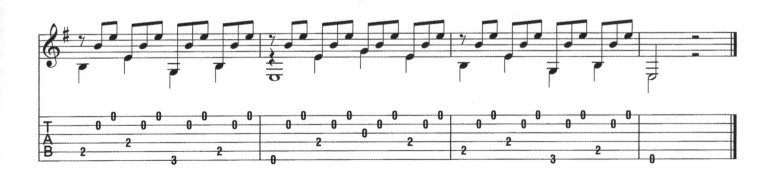

Robin Is to the Greenwood Gone

Thomas Robinson
(flourished 1589–1609)

47

Andante

48

Fernando Sor

Welscher Tanz

49

Hans Newsidler
(1508-1563)

Etude

50

Fernando Sor
Op. 60, No. 20